Anthea Gr

As one of Australia's leading experts on healthcare management, Anthea Green advised governments, directed research and managed hospitals.

But then Anthea became sick herself. Demanding jobs, single parenting and an hectic pace all took their toll... and at 40-plus her body was changing.

Good medical care allayed the illness, yet that was not enough. She needed to do more herself to restore her energy and stay well.

She had to look at the reasons she'd become ill in the first place, and then take on the responsibility herself for getting well, using all the available expertise, information and options.

This started Anthea on a long journey of exploration, into the effects of the emotions on the mind and the body, into the way the mind can drive the body onwards and upwards, and into the simple principles of 'powering-up' for a healthier, fuller and more vital life.

Anthea is now much healthier, both physically and mentally... and happier.

Driven on by her three affirmations of life: 'Enjoy the moment,' 'Never say never' and 'I can do anything that I really want to do', she believes that the answer to better living lies within ourselves.

All we need to know is how to tap into that inner energy and peace.

'Western medicine gives us brilliant diagnostic skills, surgery, intensive therapies and treatments,' she says.

'Eastern medicine, on the other hand, gives us traditions for prevention of illness and methods of healing.

'Each views the body differently. We can gain so much when we draw on the best of both, where they can work in harmony.'

Anthea, formerly the general manager of the Royal Hospital for Women, and senior policy advisor to the NSW Minister for Health, is now a consultant in healthcare management to Blackmores and is also an account manager for Carlson Marketing Group (a world-wide company in Australia).

She passes on the knowledge she has gained, both from her distinguished background in the health industry and her personal experience, to keep on 'powering up'.

Sue Williams

Sue Williams is a high-profile freelance journalist, writing features and opinion columns on everything from nuns to nudity, streetkids to movie stars, politicians to tax inspectors.

Through her strong beliefs she's earned a large following, among both people who admire her outspokenness, and those who abhor it. She is often called upon to defend her stance in radio shows. Talkback hosts regularly call for her dismissal.

She first became interested in alternative healthcare when she fell ill two years ago and conventional medicine could offer no answers.

Since learning many of the lessons of this book, Sue's been in great health.

'It takes such a little effort,' she says, 'for such great rewards.'

To

Rupert, Catherine, Michael & James,

with many best wishes for a happy — and healthy — life.

Love, Sir William

1994

POWERING UP

ANTHEA GREEN
WITH SUE WILLIAMS

PAN
AUSTRALIA

First published in 1994 in Pan by Pan Macmillan Publishers
Australia
a division of Pan Macmillan Australia Pty Limited
63–71 Balfour street, Chippendale, Sydney
In association with Selwa Anthony

Reprinted 1994

National Library of Australia
cataloguing-in-publication data:

Green, Anthea, 1947–   .
Powering Up

ISBN 0 330 27252.7

1. Stress management. 2. Stress (Psychology). 3. Conduct of
life. I. Williams, Sue, 1959 (Apr. 2)-. II. Title.

155.9042

Typeset in 12/15pt Times Roman by Post Typesetters

Printed in Australia by McPherson's Printing Group

Disclaimer
The authors may give opinions and make general or
particular statements in this book regarding potential
changes of lifestyle habits.
You are strongly advised not to make any changes or take
any action as a result of reading this book without specific
advice to you from your Doctor.

For
Rob, Alexander and Philip,
my Mother and Father.
To all who have been part of the journey.
Every step can seem a difficult struggle,
yet with every struggle there is a giant step.
-Anthea

For
Jimmy and Maya
-Sue

For
Selwa Anthony
who provided the spark.
-Anthea and Sue

CONTENTS

INTRODUCTION

From the moment a jangling alarm clock startles us awake, our bodies and minds are subject to an incredible amount of stress. For those out of work, there's the constant worry of how to keep a roof over the family's head. For those who hate their jobs, there's the strain of coping with a daily grind they loathe. And for those who love their work, there's the interminable fear of losing it.

In the home, our traditional refuge, things aren't much better. Women are still expected to take on most of the responsibility for keeping up the house, even if they work too; while they may face resistance from men about taking on domestic tasks they'd never before been expected to do. More and more families break up, with single parents left to fend alone, financially and emotionally, for their children.

But as well as the day-to-day anxieties about paying the bills, making sure there's always food in the fridge, fitting in the shopping, wondering whether the kids will make it home safely from school and if they're doing their homework, technology has brought the worries of the world to our doorsteps. Conflicts in Europe and the Middle East are no longer battles fought in bullet-ridden streets and on misty mountaintops on the other side of the globe. Television and radio has brought them right into our loungerooms to confront us nightly with the casualties, the rage and the resignation.

Many of us end up worrying from the minute we get up to the moment we eventually fall asleep — exhausted from tossing and turning in bed, brooding over our problems.

A little pressure, of course, is a wonderful thing if it makes us face up to our troubles or spurs us on to accept challenges, stretch ourselves and achieve greater heights. Too much, however, is destructive. It can lead to irritability, poor sleeping habits, a lack of concentration and, at the other end of the scale, high blood pressure, ulcers, heart attacks and mental illness. At worst, it can kill.

This clear, easy to read book is all about how to recognise stress when it's happening and what to do to keep it under control.

Indeed, if such stress can be properly managed, then it can be transformed into a powerful, positive force to drive your life onwards — and upwards.

The key is understanding our emotions; problems we may have in the way we react to people or situations. Once we learn to handle these emotions, then we are on the threshold of building a better, healthier life. If the emotions are the gearbox of our lives, then the mind is the motor. If we want to change, we can, simply by working on the conscious and subconscious parts of the mind.

Rest, in this process, is vital. Everyone knows the importance of physical rest to good health, but what about resting the mind? A few minutes reserved every day for some simple meditation or relaxation can provide astounding results.

The role of physical contact in 'powering-up' the mind and body is also critical. Overseas, massage is used extensively to help the healing process. It's still in its early stages in Australia.

One obstacle women have to face in their quest for a healthy body and mind is society's tyrannical preoccupation with youth and body image. It's easy for self-esteem gradually to be eroded. Accepting your body and aiming for health and vitality rather than some 'ideal' shape is crucial in living a happy, fulfilled life.

Of course, if you are sick, seek medical advice. If you feel you can't cope, get professional help. But to power up on health — and keep powered up — this book will really show you the way.

And your body will help you in this journey. Learn to pick up the signals your body is sending you and understand how to act on them.

The results will amaze you.

1
WHAT IS PRESSURE?

Stress has become the buzzword of the decade. We all suffer it. We all struggle to cope with it. And, as science reveals what a terrible impact it has on our mental and physical health, stress is increasingly something we all fear.

So what is stress? What causes it? And how can we combat it?

The first thing to realise is that stress, or a sense of unmanageable pressure, isn't always bad. It can be turned around and used as a positive force in your life. **Pressure turns carbon into diamonds.** But only if you know how.

THE POWER OF POSITIVE PRESSURE

Children learning to walk will stagger and fall, then stagger and fall again. But they won't give up, nor will they be punished by their parents for failing. Instead, they'll simply keep on trying until they finally manage to make those first few hesitant steps.

For most of us, learning to walk and talk will be our first encounter with pressure to achieve. Yet the way we faced it as children was totally different from the way we view it as adults. Then, it was fun to try something new; it didn't matter if we couldn't manage it first go. Our parents were always gently encouraging, filled with the confidence that, eventually, we'd succeed.

But too often in our adult lives, pressure is seen from the outset as something to be dreaded and feared. If we don't succeed at first, we'll immediately feel failures. Then, when we finally make it, our success is rarely celebrated.

Certainly pressure can be a negative force, but often, with the right attitude and preparation, it can offer a real spur to success.

Sportspeople welcome the pressure of a big event to push them to greater and greater heights. Stage and screen stars admit that first-night nerves invariably sharpen their performance. And business executives dealing in the world of multimillion-dollar deals say they're given the edge when the stakes are high — and the pressure is on.

The secret lies in being ready for the pressure when it comes.

Top-class athletes train for hours each day, stick to rigorous diets, make sure they get plenty of sleep, and discipline their minds to cope with the moment the countdown on the racetrack begins.

Hepthathlon champion Jane Flemming says: 'The best way to cope with the stress is to know you've covered every aspect that you can control of your performance.

'When you've done that, you know there's then no point in worrying about the things you can't control. If you're not in the best lane, or it's windy, there's nothing you can do. But just make sure you've controlled the controllables — that's my philosophy in life too.'

In business, the companies that most easily survive the pressures of a recession are the ones that are best prepared. They're lean, mean and have built up a loyal workforce who are willing to put up with short-term hardship in the hope of rewards to come in the future. They adjust to their environment and find a winning strategy.

TURNING THE PRESSURE ON AND OFF

An important part of all that preparation is, however, knowing when to work hard and when to give ourselves a break.

Athletes will suffer burnout if they over-train, performers will lose their flair if they don't take time out and businesses will be hit by low morale if they put too much pressure on employees.

For individuals, learning about our own capacity to cope with pressure and recognising our limits is a critical stage in the process of turning stress into a positive force. We need to know when the stress is getting too much, and learn how to get rid of it, so we can go back into that difficult situation refreshed, replenished and ready for more.

Traditionally, our remedy for stress over-load has always been to relax in the evenings after work, to make the most of weekends, or to take holidays during the year. But today those periods are no longer enough, and often not even available. We have to find new ways of dealing with the crippling burden of all the pressure we're all now under.

In the workplace, for instance, pressures are immense. The recession has meant there's no room for slack. Everyone's expected to work harder and longer to keep their employer in business — and themselves in a job. Some end up hating their work, others are forced to take pay cuts to stay with them.

But the unemployed don't have an easy time of it either. It's a strain to make ends meet. Some lose their self-esteem; others feel embarrassed at having to accept social security benefits. They are all frustrated at having to deal with government bureaucracies and big organisations to search for work and get paid. It's easy for both self-esteem and hope for the future to drain away.

In the home too there may be little relief from the stresses of the outside world. With record numbers of marriages breaking up, yet with many couples unable to afford divorce — or even the cost of living separately

— the tension can be unbearable. Add to that the difficulties of raising children and looking after rebellious teenagers or aged and dependent relatives, and homes can end up far more pressured than anything encountered outside.

There is also the strain of shifting gender roles and expectations. Many women will be feeling the strain of running what is effectively two careers: working at a job and maintaining the home. Friday nights herald a weekend of household chores. For men, there will be greater and greater pressure to play a more major role around the house.

Thus there's an urgent need actually to do something *positive* to break this stress cycle rather than merely expecting it to vanish with a weekend break.

In our youth, our minds and bodies were more resilient; we could work all day, party all night, shamelessly overindulge and still remain healthy. But as we get older, it's more and more important to be able to recognise when the stress is simply becoming too much — and work out what to do about it.

RECOGNISING OVERLOAD

When you are under too much stress you might be affected by any one of a number of physical and mental symptoms:

Physical signs
* tightness around shoulders and neck
* restricted and shallow breathing
* tightness around the chest
* increased heart rate/palpitations
* high blood pressure
* feeling of nausea
* ulcers
* indigestion/diarrhoea/constipation
* headaches/migraines
* asthma
* low sex drive
* low levels of energy or constant tiredness
* recurring illnesses
* weight loss/weight gain
* eczema
* dependency on alcohol/cigarettes/drugs

Mental signs
* frequently agitated and worried
* being on the edge of tears all the time

* inability to sleep/sleep disturbance (waking up at 2 a.m. or 3 a.m.)
* low-level depression
* a sense of being overwhelmed by life
* not wanting to get out of bed or leave the house
* poor work performance
* a sense of not being 'yourself'

(If you show any of these signs, consult your GP)

Eventually you might find relationships turning sour as you take the stress out on your partner or families. You can end up feeling tired all the time, listless and miserable. Then, to try to cheer yourself up, you might drink too much, eat too much, smoke too much or even try a few drugs — which will only compound the problems.

The whole thing becomes a vicious circle. As you feel more and more that you can't cope, you won't be able to. Finally you lose sight of any way of climbing out of the morass.

As you dig yourself deeper and deeper into a pit of unhappiness, the more vital it is that you stop, realise what you're doing and then make a definite decision to break the cycle.

However, if you've ignored all the physical

and mental warning signs, stress will actually
MAKE you grind to a halt anyway. You will
reach a point where you just can't function.

That is the time you are forced to take a break
and make an honest assessment of your life, the
way you're living it and what you can do to
make sure you have a quality future at all.

BREAKING THE CYCLE

It's vital that we find a way of breaking the
downward spiral of stress. You should look at
strategies you can use daily, weekly, monthly,
even yearly, to ensure you stay in peak
condition.

There are a number of methods of doing
this. They are part of both short and longterm
routines, and include sorting out unresolved
emotions, managing the mind, certain forms
of exercise, mental rest and touch therapy. All
are dealt with in detail in subsequent chapters.

WORK OUT YOUR OWN TRADE-OFF

Many people reading this will say, 'That's all
very well and good, but I don't have the time
to spend doing all these things to lower my
stress levels.'

That is foolish. They may believe they don't

have the time to reorder their day and make new priorities but, in reality, they can't afford *not* to. Everyone works better, plays better and loves better when they're not tangled up and torn apart by stress. A little time out every day to cope with the pressure will reap untold dividends throughout the rest of your life.

Everyone has to find their own trade-off.

Sure, it's not easy. To build a great life, full of power and energy, you have to give up something. It will demand a little bit of time out of each day and a fair amount of self-discipline. But it's certainly worth the sacrifice.

The tougher the going gets out there, the more you have to do for yourself.

RECOMMENDED READING: *Leadership Is An Art*, by Max De Pree (Dell Publishing); *Leadership When The Heat's On*, by Danny Cox and John Hoover (McGraw-Hill Inc); *Real Magic*, by Dr Wayne Dyer (HarperCollins); *Awaken The Giant Within*, by Anthony Robbins (Simon & Schuster); *The Ten Laws of Leadership*, by Bill Newman (BNC Publications); *The Mark of a Millionaire*, by Dexter Yager and Ron Ball (Internet Services Corporation).

2
MANAGING
THE EMOTIONS

In order to deal effectively with stress, we need to know what causes it.

The biggest stress we ever face is ourselves. If we're happy, then any additional pressure is easy to cope with. If we're not truly happy, then it may be enough to push us over the edge.

THE HAPPINESS FACTOR

A number of rabbits were once fed large amounts of cholesterol to test its toxicity. One by one the rabbits slowly died — except for one group. The scientists were mystified. Despite the poison, this group showed not the slightest sign of illness.

After a few weeks the puzzle was solved. Every time the rabbits were fed, their care-taker patted them, played with them and spoke softly.

From this, the scientists were able to con-clude that the positive effects of love and affection far outweighed the toxicity of their food.

For humans the process seems to be the same. If a person is happy, peaceful and calm, then their overall health will be good or improving and their ability to cope with toxic doses of stress will be high.

Some doctors believe that a person's emo-tional state actually changes the physiology of their body. To judge whether someone is likely to face chronic ill health in the future, patients are asked two questions: Do they have a purpose in life? And how do they rate themselves on a scale of happiness from one to ten?

If the answer to the first is 'No' and a low figure is given to the second, then that person is believed to be at much greater risk than someone who does have a life purpose and is happy.

All the technological and diagnostical

wizardry the West can summon up is perhaps not as accurate a predictor of the likelihood of ill health. State of mind is emerging as a key factor.

Another aspect of our lives on which our emotional state is known to have a great effect is our level of vitality. These days, for many people, that's the single most worrying problem: tiredness. Any normal, happy, healthy person should have huge reserves of energy and vitality, which even age shouldn't deplete much. There are plenty of elderly people whose vigour and verve could leave their grandchildren standing.

Look at Colleen Clifford, for example, a giant in the world of Australian showbusiness, still planning new one-women plays, TV appearances and musical evenings at the grand age of ninety-four. The secret of her energy levels is simple: 'Don't worry about the pressure of time or the onset of old age,' she says. 'Live for the excitement of each day. Everything is interesting if you think about it!'

Then there's Margaret Whitlam, wife of former prime minister Gough, whose voracious appetite for life has always left everyone else far behind. In 1992, at the age of seventy-two, she even embarked on a new career — a travel guide, hosting cultural tours of Europe.

'I have no intention of getting out of harness until I'm dragged out,' she says. 'They'll have to drag me out like a dead horse when they want me to stop.'

Lack of energy is little to do with the ageing process or with anything external. While anyone feeling depressed or short of energy is recommended to go to their local GP for a check-up, it's probably unlikely their doctor will find any obvious physical cause. And that's because the answer is inside of you.

If you are not happy with your life, have no clearly defined goals and are confused, then you'll be under considerable emotional stress. As a result, your energy levels will drop dramatically, drained by the internal turmoil.

Top US personal development trainer Lynda Wooding has made a special study of this phenomenon, particularly amongst women. She believes that up to ninety per cent of women are suffering from a lack of vitality — and it's simply because so many are leading unfulfilled lives.

'Women are brought up being taught *not* to

ask for what they want,' she says. 'It starts from the time we are little girls. We are taught to play the meanest game there is, which goes: "Be nice. Don't say what you really mean. Be nice. Don't ask for what you really want." So we spend the rest of our lives seeking approval and trying to be nice, rather than fulfilling our expectations and living our lives. We end up frustrated, angry and sad.'

Too many women end up living their lives for other people, for their parents, for their partners, for their children. They rarely stop and ask themselves, 'What do *I* really want?' — until it's too late to do anything about it. Then, to cope with their own dissatisfaction, they take on a kind of numbness, a distance, a way of no longer feeling the pain.

Men's mechanisms for dealing with emotional stress are different. They step outside their lives, distancing themselves from the situation they feel unable to face. Often you'll hear women saying that a husband or boyfriend is distant, uninvolved. It's simply the male version of numbness.

So, for both women and men, the tension of unresolved emotions builds up and up. If they still choose to do nothing and indeed try to block out emotions by becoming distant or numb, then their relationships will suffer. They'll feel even more miserable and low.

In the end, all that pain, hurt, anger and frustration will become an emotional time bomb, ticking away in their soul. The consequences of this can prove disastrous. In the same way that happiness makes healthy cells, negative emotions can leave a person dangerously vulnerable to sickness and disease.

We are only now beginning to understand the link between emotional stability and the immune system. Research on the links between the progress of Aids, the strength or weakness of the immune system, and the state of mind of the patient have taught us many valuable lessons.

Director of the Australian Centre for Immunology, Professor Ron Penny, says there have been a number of studies which prove a correlation between physical and emotional stress and changes in the immune system. One of the first, conducted in 1977, looked at people whose partners had just died. There were definite changes in their immune systems as a result of the misery of bereavement.

And while it's not yet possible to prove a definitive link between stress and disease, many people in the field believe it to exist.

'People do emphasise the benefits of stress management on a variety of diseases and we think it does them good,' says Professor Penny.

'But it is hard to prove. There are long, on-going studies being undertaken attempting to answer a question which, in the public arena, doesn't seem to need proof.'

HOW DO YOU KNOW WHEN YOUR EMOTIONS ARE HARMING YOU?

There's a very simple rule of thumb to determine whether your emotions are out of kilter: Do they regularly take you by surprise?

Do you get angry at trivial things that really shouldn't bother you? Are you more tearful than usual? Do you become afraid in situations that normally wouldn't scare you? And are you more nervous about ordinary, everyday things than you should be?

These can show themselves in a variety of ways.

All of us, as children, have seen adults explode with anger because of something trivial such as a little milk spilt on the kitchen floor. We've heard about people who start to panic when they're standing in a crowd of people. We know women who cry far more than they should at a teary movie.

These people all have a lot of emotion pent up inside. When finally there's an opportunity for release, it all comes rushing out. The reaction, as a result, will be far out of proportion to the occasion.

But if this happens to you, don't panic. Instead, welcome it. It is a clear sign that your emotions are out of balance and therefore gives you an opportunity to do something about it before anything more serious happens.

And if you are already ill, this could well prove a signpost to help you regain your health.

What do you do?

You have to find a way of constructively releasing, without doing harm to yourself or others, all that pent-up emotion.

In days gone by the head of a family would take a lead, the local priest could offer advice; and in tribal societies there were rituals and ceremonies for providing avenues for relief and release.

However, today, that kind of help is no longer readily available for most people. Sometimes friends may listen, but more often than not they don't want to, or can't, because they have their own concerns. Instead, we've learned to rely either on ourselves or simply to bottle it all up.

If you're alone, try something simple: live your emotions out loud. If you feel very angry, yell and scream into a pillow or in the car as you drive on your own. If you feel very hurt and sad, find an isolated spot and howl. You'll be amazed how much better you feel letting it all go.

Laughter is also a wonderful medicine.

In 1964, an American named Norman Cousins fell ill with a serious, degenerative, collagen disease. In a bid to improve his condition he decided to try to cheer up — and see if his body responded.

He persuaded nurses to bring old films of 'Candid Camera' and Marx Brothers movies into his hospital room. When his laughter brought complaints from other patients, he moved into a hotel and surrounded himself with comedy videos, comics and joke books.

Slowly but steadily his health improved. A doctor was called in to examine him before and after big doses of laughter. 'I was greatly elated by the discovery that there is a physiological basis for the ancient theory that laughter is good medicine,' says Norman, who has since recovered.

Now, in the US, stress-releasing humour is a growing industry. Some hospitals have set up special 'humour rooms' where patients can relax and read funny books and watch comedies on video. For the past twenty years there has been serious research on the link between humour and mental and physical health.

In Australia there are comedy acts who visit children in hospital and also groups of cancer patients, but the approach is still relatively novel. However, counsellor Kim Davis, who runs humour workshops in Sydney, predicts that it won't be long before it really takes off.

'It's all about taking another perspective,' says Kim. 'Stress is all about how you look at the situation. If you can look at the lighter side of life, through a comical viewpoint, then stress build-up doesn't seem to be quite so bad.'

In her workshops people look at attitudes to laughter. When we're four years old, we laugh four times an hour. But later in life laughter becomes almost taboo. We're told 'It's not a joke', 'Grow up!' and that people who laugh all the time are crazy and lack intelligence.

Kim's students are then taught how to laugh more. They think about how their favourite comic character might handle a particular stressful situation or they substitute different people's voices for the ones telling them about deadlines.

Playing sport and exercise can also be a great way of clearing your system, as can playing loud — or soothing — music, dancing, gardening or simply spending time with pets. In jails, where there are enormous reservoirs of undirected anger and misery, psychologists have found that introducing animals significantly lowers the levels of stress of inmates.

Otherwise, it may be time to turn to professionals for assistance. There is now a great number of proven and well-established psychotherapeutic techniques that lead people through the process of resolving emotional problems. If you feel you need assistance, contact a GP, counsellor, a psychologist, a psychiatrist, a hypnotherapist or recognised personal development trainers. Their techniques are all well respected and they can refer you on to other experts if necessary.

You don't have to feel very, very bad before you ask for help, either. People simply suffering from a lack of energy might really benefit. Psychologist therapist Jytte Beauman sees women every day who don't realise they're suffering low-level depression.

'There are definitely a lot of women around suffering from low-level depression,' she says. 'They don't realise that; they just say they're not sleeping well or they're feeling anxious or not performing well at work or drinking too much.'

But when that depression is shaken off they're generally astonished at how much better they feel. Energy comes flooding back into the body, they feel stronger and they'll have a new contentment and excitement about the future. Even more importantly, they feel in control and able to deal with the world.

THE POSITIVE SIDE OF EMOTION

If you're feeling bad, as we've seen, those emotions can drag you down, prevent you from reaching your goals and eventually result in ill health.

By the same token, if you're feeling happy, you'll have high levels of energy.

Feeling positive about life is one of the greatest forces anyone can possibly harness.

Just look at Australian adventurer James Scott, who survived forty-three days in a Himalayan cave with only snow and two chocolate bars to keep him going. It wasn't the chocolate that proved the difference between life and death, it was his desire to live.

Or what about the elderly lady whose son became trapped under his car when the jack slipped? She could see he would suffocate to death in minutes. So, without a second's thought, she grabbed the bumper and held up the car long enough for him to crawl out. As soon as he was clear she dropped the car, all strength lost. It wasn't a test of her physical ability; it was pure kneejerk emotion — her love for her son — that gave her the strength to lift that car.

Your attitude charts your life: positively up or negatively down.

If you want to be sick, you can program yourself to be sick. Plenty of people do that every day. People can and do, choose to die.

The flip side is that you can also program yourself to be well and to live longer. What you want to do, you can. What you *feel*, you are.

So, if you can sort out any unresolved emotions and be clear about your purpose in life, then you are more than halfway to achieving a strong defence against stress and ill health.

You will find you have a great deal more energy, a far more positive attitude and a wonderful sense of wellbeing. Then, when the pressure piles on, you're ready.

RECOMMENDED READING: *Quantum Healing* and *Perfect Health*, by Dr Deepak Chopra (Bantam Books); *Anatomy of an Illness*, by Norman Cousins (Bantam Books); *Pulling Your Own Strings*, by Dr Wayne Dyer (Avon Books); *Grow Rich While You Sleep*, by Ben Sweetland (Prentice-Hall), *The Healing Brain*, by Robert Ornstein and David Sobel (Papermac).

3
MANAGING THE MIND

The mind is the powerhouse of healthy living. It is the body's ultimate master control system.

What's in your mind will drive your body, your feelings and your life. If your mind's full of negativity, then your life will turn out pretty much the same. But if you truly believe you can do anything, achieve anything and be blissfully happy and perfectly healthy along the way, then your life will be brimming with success, fulfilment and joy.

But in order to properly harness the power of the mind, you must first have an idea of how it works.

IN TWO MINDS

There are two parts to the mind: the conscious and the subconscious. Research over the years has shown that the mind is like an iceberg — there's a little bit you can see above the water, and a huge amount you can't see underneath.

The little bit you can see is the conscious mind, about ten per cent of the total. Ordinary people use about four to five per cent of that part, a genius uses five to six per cent.

The other ninety per cent of the mind is made up of the subconscious. This is the part that determines most of what we do, even though most of us have no idea how to access it and use it deliberately.

Most of the important belief systems, memories, habits, personality and self-images we live by are laid down in our subconscious mind by the time we're seven years old. So what happens during our childhood can affect the rest of our lives.

For instance, if a child loses a parent when very young, that experience could easily spill over into adulthood. In that case a young girl might grow up believing, subconsciously, that if someone loves her, they'll leave her. However much that woman tells herself a relationship is for keeps, there may be a little voice inside her saying, 'No! He'll go. Just you wait and see.' She might even end up driving him away with her lack of confidence in his staying power.

This clash between what the conscious mind thinks and the subconscious mind believes can often lead to problems. Someone might have been striving for years to achieve certain goals but never quite seems to make it. Someone else might do everything they can to attain good health and a sense of wellbeing, but always ends up feeling below par.

In their cases, they're probably doing all the right things — but their subconscious is acting as saboteur.

The small businessman wants to make a success of his enterprise, but his subconscious mind is telling him, 'You're no good at business. If you expand, you'll risk everything... and probably lose it.' An overweight woman wants to slim down but a voice urges her, 'Go on, have an ice cream. You'll never lose weight, anyway. What difference will it make?'

For anyone to succeed, it is vital to get the two levels of thought working the same way. And to power up both.

POWERING UP THE CONSCIOUS MIND

To be fit, healthy and strong, you first have to *think* fit, healthy and strong. It sounds simple, but it's surprising how many people overlook this crucial step.

Unfortunately, very few people come out of their youth with a totally positive attitude to life. Instead of believing they can achieve anything they want to; tackle any goal; be warm, lovable people; and that the world is a great place, often they think quite the reverse. They believe there are few things in life they could do, that people are more likely to dislike them than like them and that the world is full of doom, gloom and disaster.

If you think that way, it will be a self-fulfilling prophecy. How you see the world determines how you will experience it. If your mental framework interprets an event as a setback, and another person sees it as an opportunity, which one will end up in the best position?

There is now a mass of evidence to show that if you have a positive, forward-looking, optimistic view of life, then your experience of it will be precisely that. If, on the other hand, your attitude is negative and you are always looking for things that can go wrong, then that will be your lot.

It is therefore critical to turn your negatives into positives, your 'can'ts' into 'cans' and your 'buts' into dust.

The most fundamental thing that will help you achieve is to find a sense of purpose in terms of your dreams and aspirations. Hope is one of the most important incentives in our lives. For the athlete, it might be the aim of one day going for gold. For the artist, it might be the ambition of a place in the Australian Opera. For the businessperson, it's that dream of clinching the mother of all deals.

We all need something to work towards, to aspire to, to spend time dreaming about, even if it's just a small promotion at work or giving the kids a Christmas to remember. Once you have a place to head for, then the journey looks a great deal clearer.

To work out your final destination, sit down with pen and paper and imagine yourself healthy, happy and doing exactly what you want to be doing in five years' time. Write down what it is and how it feels. Similarly, look at relationships. What do you want in your friends and in a partner? Once you've worked that out yourself, it will be much easier to make decisions in the future.

With that positive image in your mind it will be much easier to deal with the negatives along the way. The negatives that do drift into your mind will be overwhelmed by the brightness of the bigger picture.

And to keep that glow, celebrate every little win along the way to show yourself there is progress. If you cook a good meal for a friend, pat yourself on the back that you've made your relationship that bit richer. If you do a good job that day at work, accept compliments graciously because it's one more step towards that promotion. Revel in Mother's Day and enjoy the celebration of your contribution to your family.

Now you've made your conscious mind work for you, rather than against you, it's time to make sure the subconscious mind is thinking positively too.

POWERING UP THE SUBCONSCIOUS MIND

As we've said before, *you* are your mind. And your life, health, wealth and happiness are all a result of what your conscious and subconscious dictate. Other people don't even need to hear you speak to get an impression of you. What's going on in your subconscious is often relayed to them by the clothes you wear, your body language, the 'invisible price tag' of what you think you're worth.

All that work to keep your conscious mind working positively will be for nothing if the subconscious 'chatter' is undermining it. Instead, we need to tap into the enormous resources of the subconscious mind and push them into alignment with what the conscious mind is doing. The combined firepower of the two will provide you with virtually limitless reserves of energy to power up — and keep you powering on.

Although there are many things we still don't know about the subconscious part of the brain, we do have some tools for finding out what messages it is giving out, and how to change them. There are a number of ways to do this:

* Mind those maxims

Write down all the sayings you live by, such as 'money is the root of all evil', 'children should be seen and not heard', and so on. Don't think about them, just list them quickly; let them flow.

When you've finished, look at what you've written. They are all the messages that have been received, usually from parents, and distilled into your subconscious over the years. If there are maxims there you don't agree with, write out the reverse over and over again. That's a way of reprogramming your subconscious, to replace negative beliefs with attitudes that will positively help you.

* Handing over

Put a pen into the hand you don't usually write with and write down what you think about life, your goals and your potential. This may feel strange but it can have astonishing results.

By writing with the opposite hand, you are accessing the other side of your brain: the creative, intuitive, emotional side that is rarely listened to. This exercise will tell you what your subconscious is saying on a whole range of issues.

A person might, for instance, write with their usual hand that they want a loving, fulfilling relationship. With their other hand they might write that they're scared, that they don't think they deserve it, that they're not good enough.

This method is also useful in helping you set goals. You might think you want a high-pressured job which will leave little space for anything else. But you might actually discover you'd prefer more time with the family.

* Seventy times seven

This is an exercise devised and taught by Sydney self-development trainer Michael Rowlands. If there is something in your life that's not working, this is a powerful technique for change.

Write out a statement, tightly worded and fairly simple, which you'd like to adopt for your life. It could be something like, 'I am going to have a fulfilling and loving relationship with one person for the rest of my life', or, 'I am going to be fit, well and free from illness from this moment on'.

Then immediately write down the first thing that comes into your head uncensored.

Sometimes there may be nothing. Sometimes there may be a response. Write it down, whatever it is — even if it's just 'I'm bored', or 'This is stupid'. Don't censor it, don't stop to think about it; just move right on to writing out the next statement.

Do this seventy times every night for seven days.

Those responses are the chatter of the subconscious mind. At some point during the seventy times seven, however, the chatter will change. Your response will start agreeing with the statement, and reconfirming it. The conscious and the subconscious will have become aligned.

* Picture this

Visualisation is a technique now being recommended by many people. It is used for healing, for getting rid of stress, for relaxing, for creating wealth and promoting a real sense of wellbeing.

It involves building up a mental picture of some goal you want to attain or the person you'd like to be. The more you desire this image, the more concrete and detailed your picture should be.

If you want good health and an attractive body, your image has to be very, very clear, down to the last detail. If you want to relax, you should imagine the most tranquil of scenes to the last swaying palm and rustle of leaves.

Your picture can be as big or as small as you want. You can visualise yourself performing brilliantly in tomorrow's exam or running the country in five years' time.

You can even try to draw your picture, and pin up copies on the noticeboard, by your bed and on the fridge, so every time you see it, it becomes more vivid.

To make the visualisation even more powerful, attach feelings to the image. Add how you would *feel* when you are fit or fully relaxed lying under a palm tree on the beach or passing that vital exam. That will make your picture real. Keep this visualisation and its associated feelings close to you all the time. Gradually, it will become real.

* Affirmations

Making affirmations is a simple exercise that involves writing out beliefs about yourself or your future and scattering them all about the house or around your workplace.

For people who suffer from low self-esteem or a poor view of their future, it has proved a very effective way of turning their attitudes around. Seeing the note, 'I am a beautiful, loving human being' so many times in different places — even if you don't actually read it — is a powerful means of reprogramming the subconscious.

You can stick the notes anywhere, too: on the sun visor of a car, on the fridge, on the bedroom ceiling, on light switches, on the bathroom mirror.

* Tape recording

Record yourself talking about the things you are aiming for, what you like about yourself, what you are doing. Then play it to yourself while you're pottering around at home, while driving, or as you go to sleep. Research has shown it's particularly powerful just before you go to sleep, so the subconscious mind can feed on it overnight.

* Sleep working

A useful way of reprogramming the subconscious is to give it topics to work on while you're asleep. The best time to set in motion a few changes in your mind is just before you go to sleep, as that's when the mind is at its most receptive.

As you begin to feel drowsy, tell yourself you're a beautiful, attractive person and that your life is full of happiness, energy and vitality. Imagine it and think it again and again before you drift off. As you sleep, your mind will keep picking it up and mulling it over. It's the easiest way to make a message sink in.

* Hypnotherapy and emotional clearing
Qualified counsellors, psychologists and psychiatrists take people into their subconscious very constructively to look at past experiences and recast them. If you understand why you feel so negatively about some aspects of your life, you're halfway to being able to change.

GIVING THESE TECHNIQUES AN EXTRA BOOST

All these exercises can be made even more powerful if they're done with emotion. As you follow through any of the exercises, imagine how you'll feel when you achieve your goals.

Will you be elated, filled with confidence and overflowing with a new zest for life? Will you feel energetic, fit enough to climb mountains and strong enough to move them?

Introducing emotion will increase the potency of your vision a hundredfold.

Also, carry through the exercises with a sense of self-love. Even if your subconscious isn't yet telling you what you want to hear, make changing it a positive project.

And try to have fun as you turn your life around. Humour and laughter are great ways to make anything enjoyable and effective. Giving yourself a hard time is going to reinforce the negatives — and make the whole experience that much more traumatic, and difficult.

RECOMMENDED READING: *Succeed With Me*, by Selwa Anthony with Jimmy Thomson (Pan Australia); *Piece of Mind*, by Sandy McGregor (C.A.L.M.); *Unlimited Power*, by Anthony Robbins (Simon & Schuster); *Mind Power*, by John Keogh (Millennium Books); *Grow Rich While You Sleep*, By Ben Sweetland (Thorsens).

4
MANAGING THE BODY

The third vital element in powering up your life is making sure your body is working *for* you, not *against* you.

To do this, we need to get to know our bodies a whole lot better. Sure, we know soon enough when we're sick; our bodies show symptoms that are unmistakable. But long before we get to that point, the body is giving out signs that we should slow down, ease up or take a break. Yet we just don't hear them.

The trouble is, these days we're often actively taught *not* to take any notice of what our bodies say to us.

The most obvious example of this ignoring our own messages is when people playing sport put their bodies through an extraordinary battering — and then go back for more. If they are highly trained, fit and geared up precisely to withstand that kind of punishment, they will be fine. However, more often than not their bodies give up long before they do because they are just not prepared for that kind of rigorous and constant stress.

Most women will recognise how bad men are at listening to their bodies. Because of the macho messages they are fed from birth, many men believe that to give in to pain would brand them a wimp. When schoolboys playing sport are injured on the field, you often hear their coaches yelling at them to get up and play on, else they be thought of as not 'tough' enough to compete.

With those kind of pressures it's not surprising that we all grow up to think we shouldn't give in to our bodies when they give out a few early warning signs that there may be a problem.

Just look at the animal kingdom. Dogs or cats who feel sick slink off into the shade of a favourite tree or into a secure hiding place and rest until they feel better. We do the opposite. 'No pain, no gain' we're taught, as one of life's irrefutable maxims. 'It can't be good for you unless it hurts!'

Of course, if you're a top-class athlete in training for the next Olympics, that's all well and good. But for the rest of us, how much better it is to gently, and gradually, build up our body's strength, agility and aerobic fitness, monitoring all the way how well it's coping.

HOW CAN YOU READ YOUR BODY?

It's easy to read our body's signals when we're sick. We may have aches and pains all over, a throbbing headache, hot and cold turns, some obvious symptom of what's wrong. That's usually our cue to act; to go to a GP immediately, get checked out and treated to start the healing process.

But long before that moment, the body is giving out hints that all is not well. If only we had tuned into those signals earlier we could possibly have taken some preventative measures to head off illness before it happened or got severe.

Let me give you an example: a few years ago I was found to have high blood pressure. When I was under stress my heart would start pounding, my pulse rate would go up and I could feel the adrenalin start coursing through my body. I had a sense of being in overdrive. That was my body struggling to cope with the extra stresses and strains I was putting it through. And yet I ignored these symptoms, even though now, when I look back on it, the symptoms were all there at least a year before my high blood pressure was diagnosed.

Today I still occasionally get that sensation but now I recognise it for what it is. I know then it's time for me to have a rest, to take some of the pressure off and to give my body some exercise to shake the tension loose.

Regular exercise really helps you get in tune with your body. Once you start to work your body, you can tell when you're not quite feeling up to scratch — if your system simply feels too sluggish for exercise or if you feel nauseated or heady when you push on. You'll soon learn to read the signals more readily and more clearly.

However, on the plus side, your body will sing to you when it's feeling great, when it's healthy, energised and full of vitality. That's our aim.

UNDERSTANDING THE BODY'S LANGUAGE

There are a number of ways your body might be warning you all is not well. As we've read in Chapter Two, some messages may be symptomatic of emotional problems, others will be physical. Look out for:

* a drop in energy levels
* tightness in limbs or around the neck and shoulders
* dull pain in any area
* periods of elevated pulse rate
* periods of feeling too hot or too cold
* change in appetite
* disturbed sleep patterns
* headaches
* slight nausea or indigestion
* increased or decreased sex drive
* breaking fingernails
* dull, lifeless hair
* very dry, or unusually dry skin or rashes
* shallow breathing, coming from higher than the diaphragm
* increase in alcohol, cigarette or drug intake
* changes in the menstrual cycle, especially if

you're not on the Pill. Severe stress may even lead to loss of menstruation
* muscle twitching
* cold sores
(If you show any of these signs, consult your GP)

All of these can be indicators of some disturbance in the body, a prompt to go see your doctor or the first sign that you should take extra care of yourself.

The most immediate, and effective, steps you can take to power up your body are to improve your diet, take vitamin supplements if you need them, increase the amount of water you drink, reduce your alcohol, tea and coffee intake, draw up a moderate exercise program and make sure you get plenty of rest.

DIET

There's been an enormous amount written in recent years about what we should and shouldn't eat, not to mention the wonder diets that are to be followed with slavish obedience.

The trouble is, every couple of years the rules change. Meat is good for us, then it's bad. Dairy products are fattening, then we need them to beat osteoporosis. Eggs cause high cholesterol; now it's claimed they actually fight it.

All this can be terribly confusing, not to say disillusioning. But throughout the debates and disputes there's always been agreement on one simple axiom: that a good, balanced diet is one that contains a variety of fresh fruit, fresh vegetables, good quality protein and carbohydrate.

The best quality protein is fish; fresh produce is always better than processed; and no diet should include more than a low to moderate amount of fat and sugar. Remember, a diet low in fat and sugar also helps you to lose weight very effectively.

Follow these basic rules and you'll be giving your body the best possible head start — plus giving yourself the opportunity to feel as well as you should.

Listen to your body. Different bodies have different needs. Have a week eating a lot of protein and see how you feel. Then eat mainly fruit and vegetables for a week, and take a raincheck. Experiment. You'll soon realise what kind of diet makes you feel good and which kind leaves you a little below par.

If you do experiment, however, do make

allowances for your body's reaction to any drastic change in your diet. We are all creatures of habit. If you've been eating meat and two veg for as long as you can remember, and you suddenly switch to meals of vegetables, beans and pulses, your body may take a little time to adjust. Take that into account when you're weighing up how you feel on each different eating plan.

Yet it's not only *what* you eat, it's also *how* you eat.

To draw the most nourishment from food and to enhance the digestive process, you should try to be relaxed, unrushed and happy when you eat. Meals should be a fun, enjoyable activity to linger over and relish. Ideally they should be social occasions for all the family; a chance to take a satisfying breather together in a busy day and take pleasure in each other's company.

For many Asian, Jewish and Mediterranean people, eating is just that. The ritual of sitting down together to share a meal has a social, even spiritual, significance. Unfortunately, today, few of us have the time for this. Many of us eat on the run; members of the family may eat at different times; and we may feel we'd rather spend our mealtimes keeping up with the TV news or watching our favourite TV show. That's understandable, but it's not a good habit to get into. Try to see if you can gather all the family at the table for a meal on a couple of days of the week and make it an enjoyable tradition where you all communicate and have fun together.

On this whole question of diet, I personally love the advice of Dr John Tickell, doctor, author and athlete. For a full and healthy life, he advocates a diet of fish, vegetables, sex and laughter!

VITAMINS

Vitamin supplementation is another vexed area. With a good, balanced diet, do you really need it? The answer is: Probably yes. While vitamin supplements can't take the place of good eating habits, they can certainly boost their value.

Many of the fruits and vegetables we eat today are grown in such a way as to deplete their supply of vitamins and minerals, and they are often stored for so long that by the time they reach our plates their goodness is much diminished. Pollutants and pesticides can also be introduced to the body through food.

It's a good idea to go to a doctor who is interested in vitamins, a naturopath or a nutritionist for advice on what to take, when, and for how long. There are a number of total vitamin supplements on the market that are very good. And if you feel better on them, that's the best test of all.

'Overall they are an essential part of helping to maintain optimum wellbeing, especially for a woman who may be an over-stretched mum, a busy wife, a hard-pressed career woman or a combination of any of those,' says naturopathic consultant Rita Cozzi.

'A lot of women today are operating at sub-optimum levels. You can tell by the way they look, or the way they say they feel.'

Dr John Tickell puts it very well. He says, 'The bottom line is that go-go people who live and work in pressure-cooker environments need to eat very, very well, but usually they do just the opposite.' We all need to help our bodies along with extra vitamins when we're really on the go.

Choosing which vitamins to take, however, can be confusing as there are so many different combinations — and brands — on the market.

The industry is now being regulated to meet certain standards, but companies like Blackmores have a long and very reputable history as specialists in vitamin and mineral supplements. I have found their products to be reliable and I use a range of them. They also produce a great deal of literature on the subject, and are currently working on a book about vitamin supplementation and a history of the company.

But which vitamins to take? At different times of a woman's life, she may need varying amounts of certain nutrients. Younger women may need more of the mega-nutrients for growth and supplements of Vitamin B to help the cells adapt to the pace of change. There's also a great need for iron. Older women might do well with calcium supplements to prevent osteoporosis in later life.

When under stress, there's considerable evidence that the body needs more of these goodies. Vitamins A, C, E and B complex seem to be the ones most needed by all of us. Vitamin C is particularly helpful for fighting colds or viral infections. A, E and the B complex group are invaluable buffers against the ravages of pressure.

In addition, combinations of A, C and E are

used in anti-oxidant preparations, which are believed to counteract the presence of 'free radicals' in the body, the unstable oxygen atoms which are thought to play a part in ageing, cancer and heart disease. They are also now considered the enemy of 'bad' cholesterol. The scientific debate about anti-oxidants is confusing but it certainly adds to the argument to supplement your diet with these vitamins, particularly when under pressure.

WATER

None of us drinks enough pure, fresh water. When you think of how your cellular structure is made up of more than seventy per cent water, it's obvious why it's so important to daily replenish the water in your system. The current thinking is that we should all drink eight large, or twelve medium, glasses of water a day — the equivalent of about a two-litre bottle. It sounds a lot, but even if you just try it for a couple of weeks you'll be startled by the improvement in your skin and your digestive system and by a new feeling of wellbeing. It's difficult to drink too much.

Fruit and vegetables contain a lot of water, so if you're eating plenty of these you won't need to drink quite so much. But if you drink a lot of coffee, tea and alcohol, you'll need to drink more as these actually *deplete* the system of water. Before you drink alcohol, try to drink a glass of water, or even mix the two.

Children should be encouraged to drink water rather than always quenching their thirst with sugary juices and soft drinks. One of the best investments a family can make is in a water purifier. As well as filtering the water, it will make it taste better too — something that's always useful when there are kids about.

Water is one of the simplest, cheapest, easiest and most effective ways of giving your life a boost. It will clear your skin, cleanse your organs, reduce the harmful effects of any toxins you're eating or drinking and help gently flush illness away.

ALCOHOL

Many people find alcohol is something that gives them a sense of wellbeing and helps relax them after a pressure-filled day. It does that particularly when it is served in congenial surroundings, or with a leisurely meal. The secret is: Moderation.

For most, that means two glasses of wine,

two midis of beer or two small shots of spirits. Anything more than that is getting to a level where the benefit to the body is lost. There should also be at least three days of the week that are alcohol-free.

CIGARETTES

Anyone interested in powering-up will, obviously, not smoke.

TEA AND COFFEE

There is no doubt that too much tea and coffee is bad for the body. For people who are already highly stimulated or tense, the caffeine only pushes them further up the stress ladder. In addition, it depletes the body of the B Complex vitamins and can disturb the digestive system.

One good cup of coffee a day is therefore enough for anyone. Drink it and enjoy!

For the rest of the day, try taking bottles of purified water to work to sip from, or drink it at home. For those times when only a hot drink will do, there are a great number of alternatives. One of the best is herbal tea. There is now a wide range of flavours on the market, from exotic fruit mixes to chamomile, from orange zinger to valerian root, from peppermint to wild blackberry.

Another alternative to tea and coffee is the decaffeinated versions. Make sure they're the types, however, that are naturally decaffeinated by water rather than by chemicals.

There are also a number of coffee substitutes available in good supermarkets or health food shops. Ecco, Caro, Nature's Cuppa and dandelion coffee are all made of cereal combinations and none contains caffeine. But a word of caution: Don't expect to love them straight off if you've loved good coffee all your life. Many are an acquired taste, so don't give up if at first you're not keen.

EXERCISE

Most people these days understand the value of regular, moderate exercise.

That doesn't mean you have to run around the streets at dawn, or join strenuous — and expensive — aerobic classes. One of the best forms of exercise is brisk walking, which raises your heart rate, increases your intake of oxygen, burns fat, strengthens muscle, tones your body and gives your immune system a boost.

When you choose the form of exercise that

best suits you, make it something you enjoy, so you're sure to keep it up. It could even be a hobby like dancing.

Fitness trainer Ian English, a former decathlon champion, knows first-hand how vital regular exercise is.

'One of my favourite sayings is, "If you don't use it, you lose it,"' says Ian.

'If you don't use your mind, it becomes dull fairly quickly. If you don't use your body, your muscles will fade away and your whole system will slow down. The body was designed to move but modern society means you don't even have to get up to change channels on the TV.

'People's bodies are telling them they should be moving.'

The National Heart Foundation says people should do some kind of aerobic exercise for twenty to thirty minutes three to four times a week. And the best way to do that, says Ian, is walking, swimming or simply getting that bike out of the cupboard and taking a turn around the local park.

'We're not aiming to be superfit athletes,' he says, 'just to get moving. If we want to enjoy life and live it to the full, we need to start now.'

SEX

Sex gives us another healthy — and extremely pleasurable — way of powering up.

Putting aside all the moral and social questions about sexuality, orgasm gives the body a sense of bliss and relaxation, both of which are great therapy. Physiologically, sexual release makes the blood pulse faster through the body, which is generally recognised to be very beneficial for health and wellbeing. This is followed by complete relaxation. Psychologically, the intimacy and affection that ideally accompany lovemaking gives our emotional state a real boost.

In short, having a loving and wholesome sex life is good for your health on a number of levels — always assuming that it's safe sex.

And while it may sometimes irk women when their partners roll over and go to sleep, sex is a natural sedative for all of us. So it's pretty helpful in getting a good night's sleep too.

RELAXATION

Strangely enough, many of us are not used to feeling totally relaxed very often. Our schedules just don't allow it.

Of course, we know how it feels — probably from that time on holiday when we spent half an hour floating on our backs in the swimming pool. It felt as if we weren't tuned in, drifting around in our minds, feeling our bodies, mellow, soft and light.

But sadly, once back in the hustle and bustle of everyday life, total relaxation like that seems like an impossible dream. But it's not. It just takes a little effort.

As you relax, the chemical composition of your body actually changes. When you are stressed, you operate on a higher level of adrenalin, which allows you to work fast and hard against the odds. The body produces cortisone and endorphins, painkillers that act like morphine. The adrenalin works like amphetamines. So when people get hooked on stress, they're really getting hooked on their own 'legal drug factory'.

Relaxing can then be initially quite uncomfortable because as the adrenalin drops, the body's chemistry shifts and there is a real feeling of withdrawal. The most common symptoms are headaches, a stiff neck and tired shoulders. But as nature struggles to rebalance the body, it's best not to fight the process. Think of it as a period of convalescence, where you're nursing your body through the repercussions of periods of stress. It's enough just to be aware that the process can make you feel worse for a while before you feel better.

If you give your body a chance it will eventually embrace the wonderfully powerful recuperative time you're offering. It will sigh, relax its muscles and gradually drift off into a state of total relaxation.

And herein lies the great paradox of our bodies. When we relax and become dreamy and unstressed, we actually provide the fuel for ourselves to power up.

To power up you need first to power down.

RECOMMENDED READING: *Perfect Health*, by Dr Deepak Chopra (Bantam Books); *The Taoists' Way of Health and Longevity*, by Daniel Reed (Simon & Schuster); *Fit For Life*, by John Diamond (Angus & Robertson); *The New Pritikin Program*, by Robert Pritikin (New American Library), *A Passion For Living*, by Dr John Tickell (Formbuilt).

5
POWERING UP
ON PEACE

In the old days, scientists and philosophers believed everyone had a mind and a body, and that the two were completely separate.

Today, however, we now know that the body exists as part of the mind and that the mind drives the body. The two are consummately fused.

Even when the body falls sick, the brain doesn't rest. It instructs the body, through its immune system, to release some of the natural chemicals it stores to fight the disease.

Thus, if we're looking at how to power up our lives, it's to the mind we turn. If we can boost the mind, then that will allow the body to tap into its great resources of strength and vitality.

HOW TO POWER UP

The mind is a collection of thoughts, beliefs, memories and experiences that determine our behaviour. It is also the central control system for all that our bodies do. The mind develops patterns which sink into the subconscious, so that the next time we find ourselves in a similar situation, we'll end up reacting subconsciously.

For instance, if we believe we can't swim or run past a certain point, then the next time we try... surprise, surprise... we won't be able to. If someone gets sick when under great stress, then the next time they feel the pressure build it's likely their health will fail again. If a smoker believes she can't cope without a cigarette, then as soon as the going gets tough she'll feel that familiar craving.

The idea is to break that set of associations, to change the way we think about ourselves and our place in the world. We have to **step out of the river of memories** in order to change anything about ourselves — whether it be our health, how dynamic we feel or the way we run our lives.

The brain has 60,000 thoughts a day, and ninety per cent of those are the same as yesterday. It's like the same record playing over and over. To change it, we have to make a new recording. To do this we have to stop, let the mind rest. And then put on the record of our choice.

Meditation

One of the most potent ways of powering up is through meditation.

Meditation is the process of sitting quietly until the conscious mind stills and in its place comes the quiet of the subconscious. Some have described it as experiencing the spaces between the thoughts, like peering through the slats of a wooden platform. Others have likened it to seeing your own thoughts go past, as if watching a reel of a movie. When the chatter of the mind finally stops, there is a fundamental silence. In those moments, the mind experiences true rest and the body benefits from the shutting down of stimuli.

People who have been meditating for some time say twenty minutes of meditation gives the equivalent benefit of at least two hours of good sleep. Even for those who have been practising for only a short time, there will be a feeling of profound rest — and a sense of great energy afterwards.

The benefits are much more than simply coming out of meditation feeling refreshed. Twenty minutes twice a day — once in the morning and once in the late afternoon — will leave a person thinking clearly, with a real sense of purpose, energy and a feeling of peace. Their concentration will be better. They will be more creative. They will often find the solutions to difficult problems after and sometimes while they are meditating. They will emerge energised, revitalised and completely powered up.

Physically, the benefits are only just beginning to be appreciated by doctors, many of whom have now started suggesting meditation for patients who feel stressed or below par. There is even evidence to suggest regular meditation slows down the ageing process and many people say they feel a new spiritual peace as a result.

For those who are ill, the healing powers of meditation are formidable. By finding stillness in the mind, the body is given a breather in which to nourish its cells and mend itself.

There are many different techniques of meditation. Some have been practised since well before the birth of Christ. Today, TM, or Transcendental Meditation, is one of the most popular as it is quick and easy to learn. It involves being given a mantra — a nonsensical word with an almost musical cadence — by a qualified instructor. Repetition of the word blocks out all thought so the meditator can slip easily into stillness.

But someone trying to meditate can focus on anything that will help them into the meditative state. They might want to concentrate on a piece of music, a single thought, an image, a flower, or simply on their breathing.

How to Meditate

The simplest form of meditation is very easy and quick to learn.

1. First of all, choose a quiet place where you know you won't be disturbed. Give yourself fifteen to twenty minutes.

2. Sit in a position where you feel comfortable but also where you can hold your posture. It's best to sit in an upright chair or on

the floor with your back against the wall, as it will support you as your body relaxes. You don't have to get tangled up in some impossible lotus position.

3. Close your eyes, take a deep breath and let it out noisily through your mouth. Imagine you're letting out all the tension and stress that's in your body.

4. Sit quietly for a few moments and continue breathing slowly, in and out, in and out, releasing the tension. You're preparing your mind and body for the experience to come.

5. Then slowly sink into your breathing. Feel each breath in and each breath out. You will notice your body begin to relax as your breathing becomes deeper and deeper. Be conscious of breathing from your lower chest, your diaphragm. Listen to the subtleties of your breathing, in and out, in and out.

6. Build a fence around yourself and focus on your breathing. Don't let anything else intrude. Just push all other thoughts gently aside.

7. But don't try too hard to concentrate on your breathing. It should be easy and natural. If you find other thoughts slipping in,

don't become concerned about your inability to keep them all at bay. Just accept them, witness them and then let them go. Relax into the breath and its beautiful rhythm. **Breath is life**.

8. As you do this, be aware of the mind chatter quietening down. You will eventually experience a moment of real stillness. This is what you are aiming for.

9. After fifteen to twenty minutes, let your breathing even out. Sit quietly for a couple of minutes with your eyes closed. Then stretch your arms above your head, stretch your legs out and slowly emerge from the meditation. You may feel a little sleepy for a few minutes, but also very relaxed.

Of course it will take a period of regular meditation for you to receive the full benefit. Although you may find it difficult at first and feel it's been of no real help, after a few sessions you'll find yourself getting more and more from the experience.

It's best to meditate first thing in the morning before the demands of the day have intruded, when the air is at its freshest and you're feeling at your most calm. Then it is useful to meditate again during the late afternoon if you can fit it in, or just before your evening meal.

You can use meditation techniques in daily life. When those tense, overwhelming moments hit you from time to time — take some deep breaths, sit and relax your body for three minutes. This will calm your response, is great for the body and gives you calm control.

Try to meditate as regularly as you can. Once a month is better then never. Once a week is better still. Twice a day is perfect.

Alternatives

Not everyone needs to formally meditate to find that inner stillness. Many of us lapse into that peaceful state without even realising it — perhaps while we're gardening, doing some repetitive exercise on our own, or while we're listening to music. We won't know we're doing it but we'll have lost a sense of time, experienced the sensation of our minds drifting or have felt as though we've been in a trance. And, as a result, we'll feel refreshed and revitalised.

If that's true of you, keep right on doing

what you're doing. Different types of meditation or peaceful pursuits suit different people. If gardening three or four times a week leaves you feeling thoroughly relaxed in both mind and body, make sure you get out into the garden as often as you can. If repetitive exercise or a daily swim leaves you feeling mentally refreshed afterwards, do that regularly too. Or if simply sitting and looking at a wonderful view has the same effect, make sure you make sitting and gazing at it a habit.

Of course, it seems quite a paradox that to power up you need first to power down. But it's true. Only by relaxing the mind and slipping into a meditative state can you give your mind and body that precious time out for rest and rejuvenation. After it, you'll find your energy levels soar. Making a regular habit of meditation will power you up for the rest of your life.

Moving and Meditation

Asian cultures have great experience in meditation. Their techniques come from centuries of experience. And in addition to meditation, Asian cultures have developed yoga, tai chi and chi kung — forms of exercise which also work to release the mind.

Yoga, developed in India, teaches the power of the breath and the art of relaxation. Lessons are readily available and affordable.

The Chinese developed tai chi as a stylised form of exercise, concentration and focus. This is a very powerful combination. Like yoga, it offers exercise together with meditative relaxation. Some forms of tai chi are more martial art orientated than others — test them out.

Traditional Chinese medicine has developed forms of very specific meditative exercises designed to help heal a number of complaints. This is called chi kung — and is not readily available in Australia. In China they are getting good results in the healing of chronic diseases and in the maintenance of good health using chi kung.

Consider any of these as different options to meditation, if you can't get the hang of it. They all offer wonderful forms of exercise and relaxation and produce a sense of wellbeing. Please note these forms of exercise may not be aerobic, so keep walking briskly as well.

MAKING THE TIME TO POWER UP

This, for some people, is the hardest task of all. It's all very well *knowing* how to power up, but it's another thing actually *doing* it.

It's all too easy to skip meditation in the morning because you have to be away early for an important business meeting, or to find a reason not to sit down in the afternoon because the kids want their tea. To avoid this happening you have to structure 'down' time into your day, to make sure it's always there for you.

If you don't make sure you take a few minutes out of every day, every week and every month for rest and recuperation then it's odds on that eventually your body won't give you the choice. Very busy, pressured people need to plan some time out, once a day, once a week, once a month.

Remember: the busier and more stressed you are, the more you need to take time out to replenish yourself. In the long run, you'll be the one to benefit. Your work rate will go up, you will work smarter, you'll function far more efficiently and the time you take out will pay for itself a hundredfold in terms of your improved performance.

For women, certainly, it can be difficult to juggle maybe a career, kids and managing the home with forty minutes a day for yourself. As a single parent with a demanding career, I used to grab twenty minutes every morning between taking the kids to school and arriving at work. I'd sit in a favourite coffee shop and have a quiet cup of coffee — my one for the day — on my own. That soon became one of the most precious moments of my day, a chance to really relax, think and power up for the challenges ahead.

It's crucial for everyone to have moments alone. Even within a loving relationship, that time apart is invaluable. That time is for contemplative replenishment in your life. Finding your inner silence can be like finding peace in a turbulent storm.

In our society people constantly avoid being silent or on their own because they tend to be frightened of facing whatever needs to be faced. They never learn to listen to their body or understand what they want from life. Women especially are always too busy looking after others' needs to take stock of their own.

Time out means no social engagements,

busy shopping schedules or demanding taxi service for the children. Put aside a day, or half a day on the weekend for total relaxation, don't cook, don't answer the phone, just be. This type of relaxation time is very important if meditation or a relaxing activity is not in your schedule.

If more than this is needed every month or so, have a whole weekend of no demands... nothing. See if friends or family can take the kids.

If funds allow go away and stay somewhere restful, by the beach or in the mountains.

The message is that everyone has to adapt to what suits them. For a busy mum it might simply be sitting quietly in another room while Dad takes over the children for a while. For a businessperson it might be putting up a 'Do Not Disturb' notice on their office door for a while each day. For someone else, it might be as simple as a brisk walk first thing in the morning, before anyone else is up.

Tune in to whatever suits you best and feels intuitively right. Everyone works better, plays better and loves better when they're not tangled up and torn apart by stress. A little time out every day to cope with the pressure will reap untold dividends throughout the rest of your life.

RECOMMENDED READING: *Teach Yourself To Meditate*, by Eric Harrison (Simon & Schuster): *The Healing Brain*, by Robert Ornstein (Macmillan Publishers); *Grow Rich While You Sleep*, by Ben Sweetland (Thorsons Publishing Group), *Ageless Body, Timeless Mind*, by Dr Deepak Chopra (Rider).

6
TOUCH THERAPY

Massage is one of the oldest treatments known to humankind, and is invaluable both as an aid for people recovering from serious illness and as a precious means of powering up on health.

Its history goes back to ancient Egypt, where it was adopted as a routine medical practice. Later, the Greeks and Romans used it to treat conditions like asthma and for increasing suppleness after sport.

In the fifth century the father of medicine, Hippocrates, wrote: 'The physician must be experienced in many things but assuredly in rubbing. For rubbing can bind a joint that is too loose, and loosen a joint that is too rigid.'

Massage became imbued with various spiritual powers around the eighteenth century, when the laying on of hands was commonly thought to involve witchcraft.

Today, massage is considered an effective way of maintaining good health and is regularly used to complement conventional medicine.

A number of different types of massage have evolved from various parts of the world. Some, particularly those from the East, treat the body as a total energy system. Ill health occurs when the energy lines become blocked, so the task of the masseur is to free those obstructions. Others use the general power of touch in a variety of ways to heal and promote an overall sense of health and wellbeing.

TYPES OF MASSAGE

The most common type of massage in the West is Swedish, a system of kneading, stroking and pressing the body's soft tissues. It's a very smooth, flowing and relaxing kind of massage and is most commonly used as a form of stress relief.

On the simplest level, it increases blood

circulation to the skin, pushes oxygen and nutrients to the muscles and stimulates the lymphatic system, draining toxins from the body.

In addition, it's a wonderful relaxant. People who have massages regularly say they can actually feel the accumulated stresses of their lives being kneaded away as they lie on the massage table. It is an instant form of relief.

By relaxing the muscles and working on the circulatory and nervous system the masseur calms everything down. When people lie down on the massage table, once they are relaxed, they breathe deeper and let the tensions drain away.

While being massaged the body is being relaxed but at the same time stimulated at a deeper level due to increased circulation of blood to the tissues.

People with specific problem areas benefit from Remedial Massage which involves spot working on an injury or painful joint with pressure applied at a deeper level than with Swedish massage.

Another popular form is Shiatsu, which concentrates on small areas of the body, using pressure from the fingers, thumbs, elbows, knees or even feet to rebalance the body.

Reflexology is massage used only on the feet, practitioners believing that each point on the sole corresponds to a particular area of the body. Reiki, which originates from ancient Tibet, involves channelling certain energy forces within the body.

A lot of the benefit of massage is in the human touch, and in the feeling of being cared for.

AROMATHERAPY

Aromatherapy is an ancient form of treatment, which adds an extra factor to massage by combining a range of essential oils — the essence of plants and flowers — to the treatment.

The practice is believed to date back to about 4500 BC in China, India and Egypt. The Chinese were more interested in the medicinal uses of essential oils while in Egypt they had cosmetic applications, for processes such as embalming and spiritual rituals. Oils, such as myrrh, cypress and cedarwood were used both in Egypt and India.

In ancient Greece, Aphrodite used oils to rid

the country of plagues, doctors used them as medicine and the ordinary citizens made them to mask the terrible stench of urine in their homes. From there they went to Rome, where they were combined with massage as the beginnings of modern aromatherapy. In the tenth and eleventh centuries the Arabs were the first to properly distil the oils rather than merely soaking petals and leaves.

Aromatherapy works through the use of smell and the ingestion of the oils through the skin. The odours pass through the nasal tissues to the olfactory nerves which stimulate the hypothalamus in the brain.

This tiny organ is responsible for regulating dozens of bodily functions including temperature, thirst, hunger, blood sugar levels, growth, sleeping, waking, sexual arousal and emotions such as anger and happiness.

To smell anything is like sending a message to your brain's brain and from there to the rest of your body. Many of us know the power a smell can have in bringing back a memory complete with all the detail and the emotion.

Essential oils can be used in a variety of ways. Combined with massage they make a very pleasant and effective treatment. It can build up the immune system, balance the emotions and detoxify the body.

One of Australia's leading aromatherapists, Fiona Fanner, says the treatment is also extremely pleasant.

'It's a very subtle, nurturing treatment,' she says. 'The sense of smell and the emotional responses and the endorphins are uplifting. It's extremely powerful. People generally underestimate just how powerful.'

A lot of research into aromatherapy is currently being carried out by a number of French hospitals, while in Britain nurses are being encouraged to study the discipline. Here in Australia the number of classes available to nurses has increased. Most believe the use of aromatherapy will grow at a phenomenal rate over the next few years as a supplementary treatment for healing and the maintenance of health.

As well as having a proper treatment from an aromatherapist, which may last up to an hour and a half, people can also put a few drops of oil into a bath, or burn a favourite oil regularly at home to help them relax and unwind. It is a good idea, though, to have at least one consultation with a qualified aromatherapist to discuss which oils can benefit you the most.

'People might want to use them as a relaxant or to help a specific disorder,' says aromatherapist Louise Davis. 'It's best to have advice first to get the most out of it. Then people can use them from birth until death.'

Prices of the oils can vary, from fifty cents an ounce for the relatively common tea tree oil, to $300 an ounce for something like rose otto, which is grown for only thirty days a year in Bulgaria and requires 1000kg of petals to produce an ounce.

The most common oils used are:
* lavender — soothing and calming
* rose otto — nurturing and soothing
* cypress — astringent and invigorating
* eucalyptus — decongesting and antiseptic
* sandalwood — strengthening and relaxing
* lemon — refreshing and uplifting

THE USE OF TOUCH

In the United States, trials are currently being conducted to examine the benefits of extending the use of massage and aromatherapy. Already they're in teaching hospitals to help patients deal with pain and complement conventional medical treatments. There is even a pain management clinic in UCLA where patients are required to have regular deep tissue massage as part of their overall treatment program. In Europe too, particularly in Germany, massage is commonly offered as a supplement to drugs — to alleviate pain.

In Australia, massage has been offered to pregnant women, by midwives, and now we are seeing aromatherapists being invited into hospitals.

The amount of interest in massage and aromatherapy as healthcare tools is increasing so fast that their use is expected to rise dramatically over the next few years.

THE IMPORTANCE OF TOUCH

Massage can enhance healing, particularly in the case of an illness that affects the immune system. Therapists often find that with regular treatments there is a definite shift in the overall health of a client. This means that a patient's regular medical regime will have more effect too. If they are stronger, healthier and happier, then the chances of recovery will greatly improve.

The physiological benefits of touch can be multiplied numerous times by what the mind does as the body is being massaged. Most people drift off into a meditative state, which greatly improves the quality of the treatment. That will add a whole new dimension to the benefits of the massage itself, especially if the practitioner works with the person in a way that promotes relaxation of the body and mind. As we've already learnt from Chapter Five, moving into the meditative state is one of the most potent forces for healing and longterm health we can harness.

There is also the nurturing power of touch, the way human caring and love is communicated. Generally, in our society, people are just not touched enough. In other cultures, families, extended families and friends embrace each other regularly. The level of touching in the West, however, has been low for a long time. Many people suffer from real deprivation.

For instance, we know that newborn babies will fail to thrive and in some cases can even die, if they are not touched or loved enough. For any child, their progress in learning to walk and talk will be much slower if they are starved of affection. In other cultures, including African, South American and Indian, babies are routinely massaged during their first few months and years of life. But in the West, doctors between World Wars I and II actually advised mothers not to kiss and cuddle their babies for fear it could damage them psychologically! Thank goodness those days have now gone.

Touch can be used as an expression of love which has a powerful effect on our body's and mind's abilities to heal. As we learned in Chapter Two, people who are happy and stable and who lead loving, fulfilled lives are much more likely to get well and stay well than people who are sad, angry, frustrated or who simply feel unloved.

The combination of massage and aromatherapy can work on many levels, making a person feel nurtured and special. And when the mind feels good and the body feels great, each will work on the other to make the overall you feel full of health and vitality.

HOW OFTEN?

Many people have the attitude that massage and aromatherapy is a terrible indulgence and something they can well afford to do without. Measure that, however, against the personal cost to yourself of living your life three degrees under par. It's a real investment in yourself and a regular treatment will be a great weapon in your armoury of powering up.

Cost is often a real consideration. Pace yourself as you can. Or do a massage course with a friend and learn how to treat each other.

Women in particular often gain the most from massage and aromatherapy, as they tend to be more open about the effects. They are often the ones too who are under the most unrelenting pressure, for which touch is a marvellous and simple remedy.

If you're not under too much stress, or you're making sure it dissipates fast by powering up on all the other fronts, a treatment once every month or six weeks should be adequate. But if you're feeling a little under the weather, once a week or once a fortnight at first should do wonders for your health until you feel strong enough to make do less often.

However, do bear in mind that you may not jump off the massage table feeling fabulous. There is sometimes a time lag between a treatment and its effect, and it may even make you feel worse before you feel better because of all the toxins it is freeing from your system. The length of that time lag will depend on the level of stress you are under and how well you are coping.

After a treatment you should go home and spend a couple of hours sitting quietly until your body feels ready to come out of its reverie. After regular treatments you will feel the difference and know the benefits to your overall sense of health and energy levels. You'll be ready to take on the world!

RECOMMENDED READING: *The Tao of Health, Sex and Longevity*, by Daniel Reid (Simon and Schuster); *Love*, by Leo Buscaglia (Souvenir Press); *Perfect Health*, by Dr Deepak Chopra (Bantam).

7
BEAUTY
AND THE BEAST

Every woman, even the most beautiful, wishes constantly that her body were different in some way. It might be larger breasts she yearns for, smaller hips, a neater waist or longer legs.

But for most women now, this angst over body image has become a source of great pressure. It's not how we *feel* that's important, it's how we *look*. And when the shape of a woman's body can eventually end up shaping her attitude to herself and to her life, it's time to step back a few paces and look at just where the pressure to be perfect is coming from.

FASHION AND BODY SHAPE

If you took a stroll through the world's best art galleries, there are few women pictured who conform to our idea of the ideal size-ten figure. Instead, there are a series of alluring women, each of them curvaceous, voluptuous and fleshy.

Botticelli, Rubens, Gauguin, even Picasso, saw the perfect woman as well-rounded. In Australia, Norman Lindsay and Brett Whiteley also painted women with shapely hips and breasts.

It wasn't until the advent of the camera, in fact, that the ideal female form shifted so dramatically. For a woman to be photographed well and look good draped over the pages of the fiercely competitive fashion magazines she had to be quite tall — and very thin. Television cameras also put ten pounds onto the size of any woman. Suddenly, to be thin was not only desirable, it was positively *necessary*.

Since then, images of very thin, long-legged women have permeated our lives. In film, on TV and in every facet of the media, skinny women are presented as role models for the rest of the nation's women. Rounded women are simply fat. Indeed, if Marilyn Monroe were trying to break into the acting profession these days, she would have been told she was too fat to have made it.

Some claim this is the last power men have over women. In every other way women are gradually claiming equality and the right to achieve whatever they want in the workplace and the home. But while a woman might be successful, confident, outspoken and look as if everything in her life is under control, secretly she might still be a forlorn victim of this tyranny of body image. It doesn't matter that she's got a high-flying career, a great relationship and is in fabulous good health, if she feels she's too fat she might be miserable. This can be one of the most powerful — and destructive — factors in a woman's life.

It's not enough either to blame men for imposing sylph-like ideals on women. Often, when they're pressed, men will admit their perfect woman is one who's voluptuous with plenty of shape accentuating their essential womanliness.

Psychologist Terry Colling is an expert on

men's attitudes and he believes that men aren't seduced at all by the images of the waifs who adorn the pages of magazines.

'Most of us men find the image of the "ideal" woman flouted in magazines skinny and bony and not very comfortable at all to cuddle up with in bed,' he says.

'You'd have to put cloth around their edges to stop being scraped by their bones.

'And, obviously, men feel less threatened by a partner who's not perfect, because most men don't have the body of David and would feel very uncomfortable with a woman who looked like Bo Derek.'

He says it's more the case that women impose unrealistic images on themselves. If you showed a hundred women pictures of various body shapes, they would invariably pick the thinnest. The men would choose the bigger women with real breasts and bums.

While women can therefore be more vulnerable to the thin images of perfection they see all around them, it is, however, a phenomenon that's beginning to affect men in great numbers too. Women are becoming more critical of men's bodies, and men are far more concerned about their own body image.

Hospitals report more men than ever are seeking treatment for eating disorders, while the cosmetic surgery industry for men is experiencing a minor boom.

For good health physically, mentally and emotionally, we have to remember that how we look doesn't dictate who we are, and who we are is certainly not determined by whether or not we can fit into a size-ten dress.

LOSING WEIGHT

A survey was conducted a few years ago in Newcastle asking women how they saw their health needs. The overwhelming majority said body weight was one of their major concerns. Another survey found that there was only a handful of women who had never been on some sort of diet. These are startling findings when you consider that only thirty-six per cent of the entire population has a body weight problem, and most of that percentage is men.

So it seems weight is often perceived as a problem when it's not at all. But whatever it is, you can be sure of one thing: it's a potent source of low self-esteem, worry and misery. If you're already feeling bad about yourself, then even when you fall inside the normal weight range you'll believe you're fat, undesirable and unlovable. This will further sap your confidence, undermine your pleasure in life, reinforce your negativity and may even lead to low-level depression.

The pressure we are all under to conform to the ideal shape should be recognised as exactly what it is — a tool for selling products, whether they be new clothes, a different brand of make-up or even dreams of happiness. That pressure should not be accepted. If your body is healthy and within the normal weight range, then it's more important to be concentrating on lifting your levels of vitality, energy and happiness than exhausting yourself trying to comply with some unrealistic fad in body weight.

Healthy body weights for height should be within the following ranges, for both women and men:

Height	Weight Range
140cm (4'7")	39kg–54kg
150cm (4'11")	45kg–61kg
160cm (5'3")	52kg–68kg
170cm (5'7")	58kg–72kg
180cm (5'11")	65kg–86kg
190cm (6'3")	72kg–95kg

(supplied by the Australian Nutrition Foundation)

The message in this is to be healthy in mind and attitude and the rest will follow. If you have good levels of energy, your body weight is within the normal range and you are getting some form of exercise on a fairly regular basis, then you will look healthy and be beautiful in your own right.

If you feel good about who you are and what you are, but would still like to change your body, then it will be far easier if you do it by feeling healthy and vibrant through the positive power of the mind than if you start off by feeling depressed and down about the task ahead. And change it to the way *you* want it to be, rather than to someone else's ideal. Remember: they're either trying to sell you something or you're becoming the victim of someone chasing a fantasy.

Our beauty and our health doesn't rest merely on the size of our hips.

EATING DISORDERS

Along with the unrealistic attitudes many women develop about the size of their bodies, there seems to be an alarming rise in the number suffering from eating disorders.

Feminist writer Dale Spender, who herself

suffered from anorexia nervosa at the age of forty-two, has estimated that between a third and one half of young women in Australia today depend on vomiting and laxatives to lose weight, while anorexia is also becoming increasingly common among menopausal women. She says it's reached such a crisis point that those women who say they *don't* have a problem are the odd ones out.

While there are no reliable statistics in Australia about the extent of eating disorders — as they are often listed under a range of headings — figures show that 150,000 women died in the USA from anorexia in 1991, more than the total number of deaths from Aids. Up to eighty per cent of schoolgirls in the USA now think of themselves as overweight.

These statistics are indeed frightening, especially since we now know that when someone develops something like anorexia, they simply can't help themselves. When they look in a mirror they actually see a body that is overweight rather than seeing a body that to the rest of us might look all skin and bone.

Whether it's bulimia, where there's often a pattern of binge-vomit, or anorexia, where sufferers can end up simply starving themselves to death, such disorders tend to hinge on our own self-image and non-acceptance of who we are.

Most hospitals now have referral facilities to specialist units that deal with eating disorders, while hypnotherapy is also a popular option for sufferers.

Clinical hypnotherapist Belinda-Jane Cummings finds a third of her practice involves helping women who have developed eating disorders. She firmly believes that a healthy mind creates a healthy body. A mind that's not healthy can create its own problems.

'The subconscious mind is the feeling mind, the motivating mind and, as such, it will always win,' she says.

Most people tend to associate food with love, so depriving themselves of food is an admission that they are unlovable. Then becoming obsessed with diets and exercise programs is often a diversion from the real issue, which is self-love.

If people can be taught to take responsibility

for themselves, understand themselves and love themselves, then they'll find the eating disorder disappears along the way.

COSMETIC SURGERY

You have to question why women put their bodies through the trauma of anaesthetics and surgery in the quest for a better body or face.

Certainly, cosmetic surgery has a place where there's disfigurement from accidents, burns, congenital deformities or unsightly birthmarks. But it is a great shock for the body to deal with in return for the loss merely of a couple of inches around the hips or a few wrinkles around the eyes.

For many women the decision to go ahead with surgery comes from low self-esteem. The solution to that, however, is unlikely to be found in the surgeon's knife.

Instead, women should be focusing on feeling better, more sensual, and fitter. If you feel great, it's odds on you'll look great. And if you look great, then all ideals will pale beside your healthy glow.

RECOMMENDED READING: *The Beauty Myth*, by Naomi Wolf (Vintage); *Beyond Mateship*, by Terry Colling (Simon & Schuster); *Ageless Body, Timeless Mind*, by Dr Deepak Chopra (Rider).

8
HORMONAL HEARTACHES

From the very early teens, women's lives are driven by their hormones. The onset of puberty heralds the start of a monthly menstrual cycle, which for many may be physically painful, mentally exhausting and emotionally nerve-wracking. Pre-menstrual Syndrome (PMS) has even been quoted as a defence in murder trials, where women are said to have been pushed over the edge by their hormonal imbalance.

With physical maturity come all the tricky decisions for women that relate to their reproductive capacity. For most women there is a constant process of decision making and balancing the changes in her hormonal life.

The dilemmas of contraception, care about sexually transmitted diseases, attention to preventative health care with pap smears and regular check ups, decisions as to when to have children, have to be managed physically and emotionally.

In addition there are the changes in body, mind and feelings that come with some of those decisions, such as pregnancy, childbirth, post natal adjustment, continuing contraception etc.

While many of these things are a great joy, they require women to adapt and adjust, pushing us outside our normal comfort zone.

Swings in a woman's hormonal balance can produce big changes in her temperament, view of the world and the way her body feels.

The larger the swing the more evident this is. Some experience this most strongly after giving birth and at the time of menopause. The depression some women experience after birth is beginning to be well recognised. Medical attention must be sought.

Changes in hormones can hit with gusto as a woman moves into middle age.

There may be a period of peri-menopause, when many of the symptoms of the real thing are beginning to make themselves felt, yet without the reassurance of knowing it's truly arrived. Finally, of course, there is the menopause.

Throughout their lives, women are constantly having to make adjustments due to their shifting hormonal levels. It helps enormously to have a basic understanding of what is going on, and a healthy attitude to the changes.

MENSTRUATION

There is a lot of myth, folklore and wisdom attached to women's cycles that is handed down through cultures and generations. In some African societies women are sent out into the bush to bleed, as it's considered shameful and dirty. In others it's a time they're considered at their most desirable and 'womanly'.

Many compare the monthly changes in a woman to the phases of the moon and offer that as proof that women are much more in tune with nature than men are. Women on the Pill, however, are not so finely tuned in to their bodies as those not on the Pill. When they do eventually come off the Pill, they are usually shocked by the swings in their behaviour and body without the Pill as moderator. If they've been taking it for around ten years, they might not even remember what they were like before.

Some women have a terrible time with their periods. Hippocrates was the first to recognise the malaise: 'Shivering, lassitude and heaviness of the head denoted the onset of menstruation...' Among the symptoms women may suffer are sore breasts, headaches, bloating and agonising stomach cramps along with a very heavy loss of blood. They may also experience a wide range of mood changes: one moment euphoric, the next grouchy and irritable.

An ancient poem quoted by Simone de Beauvoir in *The Second Sex* reads:

Oh menstruating woman, thou's a fiend
From whom all nature should be screened!

Menstruation does have completely different effects on different women. One US study found that forty-five per cent of attempted female suicides took place in the week before bleeding, while other research has shown fifty-two per cent of women admitted to hospital after serious accidents were just about to start their periods.

Because of its impact on some women, PMS is gradually becoming more and more acceptable overseas as a defence in criminal cases involving women. In Britain it has successfully been used in trials as a plea of diminished responsibility for offences ranging from shoplifting to manslaughter. So far in Australia PMS has only been used as a mitigating factor. But this may soon change.

Criminologist Dr Patricia Easteal says: 'The prevailing view presented in legal journals is that a need exists for a greater knowledge about PMS and a subsequent greater acceptance within the medical community.

'As this occurs, it is likely to be raised more often in courts around the world.'

No one knows precisely what causes PMS. Theories over the years have included the production of oestrogen, progesterone, cortisone and other hormones, vitamin deficiencies, allergies, and psychological, genetic and social factors.

Regardless of the cause, how well women handle the difficult times of their cycle will depend, to a large extent, on how those problems were handled by their parents, school and, later on, their partners.

If their mothers were old-fashioned and went along with the old stricture of 'lots of bicycle rides and cold showers', then it's quite possible they'll push on through every month. If, on the other hand, they were used to seeing their mothers behave like invalids for two days each month, tucked up in bed with hot water bottles, then it's probable they'll end up exactly the same.

Professor Michael Bennett, professor of the School of Obstetrics and Gynaecology at Sydney's Royal Hospital for Women, says mothers with painful periods often have daughters with painful periods.

'We are influenced by our environment and the people we live with,' he says.

'If a mother goes to bed for a couple of days each cycle, then that gives the daughter licence to do the same.

'There are those who don't bleed excessively and don't perceive they bleed excessively and, as such, they certainly don't regard menstrual changes as being unpleasant or unfortunate.

'And there are those who do suffer, who

have painful periods and bleed like hell or perceive they bleed heavily and that does colour their outlook of themselves and their lives. I am cynical enough to ask how much is real and how much isn't.'

But understanding how and why your body is changing will help. A woman who gets a bad migraine just before her period will not have any less of a headache knowing that it's triggered by a drop in the level of oestrogen her body's producing, but she may feel better knowing her system's working well. A woman who snaps at her kids and loses her temper frequently at a certain time of the month might cope better, and go easier on herself, if she realises why she's feeling so low.

'I think, in this regard, most women are unaware of their body structure and function,' says Professor Bennett.

'I see what I think is basically a little bit of fear or fright. In many homes, where knowledge is not readily available from parents or teachers, it must be very frightening indeed. An understanding of what's going on probably does make life better.'

The biological clock is also a very sensitive mechanism. It can be easily upset by drugs, such as a general anaesthetic, or by physical or emotional stress. This can in turn lead to irregular periods or indeed women losing them altogether. Thus, if a woman can cope well with stress, then she'll cope that much better with the demands put on her by the menstrual cycle.

Primrose oil supplements, vitamin B6 therapy, Blackmore's PMT nutritional supplement, an improved diet with a reduction in the intake of tea and coffee are thought to help with PMS symptoms.

THE PERI-MENOPAUSE

The phase before the menopause can be particularly difficult as some women experience a few of the symptoms in a mild form long before they're due. These may include:

* hot flushes
* depression without reason
* anxiety and irritability
* formication (a feeling of ants crawling under the skin)
* tiredness
* insomnia
* palpitations

* vaginal dryness
* poor memory
* indigestion
* night sweats
* poor concentration
* muscle and joint aches

Often these symptoms are not readily connected with the menopause because the woman is still having periods. This can be a very frustrating phase, but it needs to be acknowledged. A woman who is in tune with her body can sense its changes all through her forties, ready for the advent of the menopause at around fifty-two.

But for most, the early signs of menopause seem to hit when we're least expecting them. Often we'll be bewildered by the symptoms. Yet if you know your body and understand the process, then you can start to manage it.

Coping with stress can be important here too. I find that when I am really stressed any symptoms I've had of the menopause get worse.

THE MENOPAUSE

This can be very traumatic for some women, signalling as it does the end of their reproductive life, which many interpret as the beginning of old age. Others look at it more constructively: as the dawning of a new freedom from the tyranny of the monthly cycle. Author Gail Sheehy calls it 'the gateway to a second adulthood'. Feminist Germaine Greer views it as a stern confrontation with death.

'There are a number of women who are absolutely delighted when they get to the menopause,' says Professor Bennett. 'A three- to four-day bleed every twenty-eight days is more than I would want to put up with. The prospect of that finishing is a great pleasure.

'But for others it's an absolute disaster. They feel they have lost that which makes them female, which makes them different.'

However well or badly women take it, it's only natural that the change is a momentous event in their lives. No other warm-blooded animal outlives its reproductive capacity to the same extent, continuing on — thanks to improvements in healthcare and advances in medicine — for around forty years after bearing children.

How well women do manage depends on a number of factors. If, for instance, they suffered terrible pre-menstrual tension all their lives and bled heavily, then the finish of the functioning of the ovaries may be more welcome than for those who rarely had any trouble.

Again, understanding the changes that are going on with their bodies is critical. If a woman can trace a symptom back to its cause, she may feel a lot more relaxed about it and therefore cope much better.

HORMONE REPLACEMENT THERAPY

HRT, small doses of natural oestrogens given to replace the shortfall in the body, is today the subject of a great deal of controversy. Some doctors hail it as the most important medical breakthrough for women's lives since the advent of the birth-control pill. Others, most notably Germaine Greer, see it as nothing more than a cynical attempt by evil drug profiteers to cash in on women's fears.

It's important therefore to look at both the pluses and minuses of the treatment before deciding whether or not to pursue it.

The pluses
Firstly, HRT lessens the risk of osteoporosis setting in so soon after the menopause. Six to eight years after the ovaries have stopped

functioning there is quite a dramatic loss of bone substance in women. A quarter of the women who go through the menopause without the use of HRT break a leg by the age of seventy. A significant number die or end up permanently bedridden as a result. Fractures of the vertebrae are also relatively common. HRT staves off brittle bones and makes a break less likely to occur even at the age of eighty.

HRT also lowers the risk of coronary thrombosis in women. Generally women are protected against this by their levels of oestrogen. Ten to fifteen years after oestrogen production has stopped, however, the risk rises. By the age of eighty, women face the same odds as men. HRT pushes the likelihood of having a coronary on ten years, to beyond eighty-five.

The treatment is useful too in helping with some of the discomforts of the menopause. Hot flushes, night sweats, forgetfulness, a dry vagina, a decrease in the libido: HRT can relieve them all.

The minuses
Its usefulness depends very much on the kind of oestrogen that is used and how it's administered. The patch applied to the skin, although

relatively expensive, has a number of very important advantages over the taking of drugs by mouth. Taken orally, the drug is absorbed into the intestine and goes through the liver, where it has the power to affect the metabolic pathways. It can occasionally cause nausea. Through the skin, it doesn't interfere so much with the rest of the system.

It would also seem that women who have received HRT in the form of oestrogen alone have an increased risk of cancer of the uterus and possibly the breast. However, there is some suggestion that women who have breast cancer and who have been on oestrogen do better than those who have never received the hormone. A four- to five-year international study is about to be mounted on the link.

'We may end up saying, I think, that in the long term HRT may marginally increase the risk of breast cancer, but if you get it, then you are going to do better than if you weren't on HRT,' says Professor Bennett.

So the decision on whether to join a HRT program is therefore a very difficult one.

Basically I would say that if the signs and symptoms of menopause are distressing to the point that your quality of life is diminished, then seek good medical advice and consider HRT. If they're not so bad that you really need intervention, then I would question the need for it.

In the final instance, your body will always tell you if it feels right.

RECOMMENDED READING: *Women's Hormone Problems*, by Dr John Eden (Royal Hospital for Women); *The Silent Passage*, by Gail Sheehy (Random House); *Menopause — You Can Give It a Miss*, by Dr Sandra Cabot (Women's Health Advisory); *Women and Crime: Premenstrual Issues*, by Dr Patricia Easteal (Australian Institute of Criminology); *The Second Sex*, by Simone de Beauvoir (Simon & Schuster).

9
PRACTISING
WHAT WE PREACH

Now we know what to do, it's just a question of getting down to doing it. At first, you might find it difficult to put everything you've learnt into practice. One day you don't have enough time to meditate; the next, you feel too tired to exercise or you binge on junk food. But if you do manage to get into a routine you'll soon look — and feel — wonderful. At that point your powering up schedule will no longer look an uphill battle. It will be something you're eager to do each day because of the benefits you're getting out of it.

The key to it all is making sure every area of your life is in balance.

'The ideal of perfect health depends upon

perfect balance,' says mind–body expert Dr Deepak Chopra.

'Everything you eat, say, think, do, see, and feel affects your overall state of balance.'

Thus it's important to get to know your body, to understand the signals it sends out to you and to learn how well it functions on different diets, types of exercise and amounts of meditation or relaxation. To know your mind is to possess the power to change your life for the better. To know your emotions means they'll never be a drag on your progress.

Try to get in tune with nature too — as far as modern city-living allows. Find a way of going to the ocean, to a park, to your garden, or to sit in the sun on a balcony where there are plants and soak up the freshness of nature. Eat foods in season and work with the climate. Don't forget our bodies are deeply tuned to the rhythms of nature.

GOLDEN RULES

* **Exercise regularly.** It doesn't have to be a fierce bout of aerobics, it can be a walk in the morning, a gentle spot of tai chi or a quiet yoga session. Early morning is always the best

time, when the air is fresher and your body's metabolism is ready to get going for the day ahead.

* **Always eat breakfast.** Your body will slow down in order to cope if it's not given enough fuel to fire it up. There's a lot of truth in the old adage of breakfasting like a king, lunching like a prince and dining like a pauper. An ideal breakfast is a wholesome, unrefined breakfast with cereal, fruit and some protein.

* **Drink plenty of water** throughout the day. Take a bottle of water to work and substitute it for tea and coffee.

* **Eat for power.** Eat a large variety of foods, as much fresh fruit, vegetables and fish as you can and plenty of raw food. Cut down on fats, sugar and over-processed and over-refined foods. Reduce alcohol to moderate levels.

* **Make sure you get plenty of rest.** You should not resign yourself to having insomnia. Sleep is vital for relaxation and healing. If you can't get to sleep at night, take a look at how you spent your evening. Watching exciting movies on TV before you go to bed might be too powerful a stimulus for your body to cope with. Or look at your levels of anxiety.

* **Meditate or power down.** In the morning, before you start your day, is a great time, but also try a five-minute break in the afternoon if you're feeling very stressed. If you choose not to meditate, try to get regular quiet times to yourself instead, when you can truly find a sense of stillness.

* **Get plenty of fresh air and sunlight.** Shift-workers need to be especially conscious of how often they manage a break outside.

* **Laugh a lot.** Surround yourself with people you can have fun with. Laughter really is a great medicine.

* **Try to have a regular massage**, anything from once a week to once every six weeks, depending on your health and stress levels and how well you're coping.

* **Once you turn forty, have a medical check-up** to get the benchmarks of your blood pressures, cholesterol, and so on. Then monitor your health and those vital signs with your GP.

* **Listen to your body signals and learn to interpret them.** When they're telling you you're sick: stop. Soldiering on usually does far more harm than good. Take time out to recuperate.

DAILY ROUTINE

Your powering up routine may seem a little daunting at first, but break it down into manageable tasks.

Try getting up just thirty minutes earlier than you normally would each day. Spend the first ten minutes on meditation or quiet contemplation, then exercise for twenty minutes. After that, shower and enjoy as calm a breakfast as you can make it. This should set you up for the rest of your powered-up day.

Continue that routine for a week. How do you feel? Later on you can easily decide to meditate or exercise for longer, depending on how you feel. But take one step at a time. Build your routine gradually over a period of time rather than trying to do it all at once. That way, it will slowly become a part of your life.

Such a routine won't suit everyone, though. Some people might prefer to be more flexible and simply find the time each day, maybe at different times, to fit in their powering up schedule. Again, everybody is different. Work out your own individual plan to suit your life and personality.

Whichever way you do it, however, make sure you give yourself a bonus for doing so well. Celebrate your achievements. If you've managed to keep up your routine for six days straight, reward yourself with a lazy lie-in on the seventh day.

And that's in addition to your other reward: a real surge of power and wellbeing running through the rest of your life.

THE KEY TO IT ALL

The message of this book is to manage your health. Take an objective look at where you're at in mind, body and spirit. Then go to work to restore health or power it up still further so you're ready to meet every challenge — and rise to every opportunity.

'Sharpen the saw,' as Stephen Covey says in *The Seven Habits of Highly Effective People.*

Look at what's happened in the past and what lies ahead.

If you're heading for a period of intense pressure and stress, put aside extra time for exercise, rest and relaxation. Make sure you're eating well and taking the right vitamin supplements. Don't wait till you have a health problem: fix yourself up NOW!

It's rather like treating your health as a bank balance. Look at the receipts and the expenditure. Make sure, at the end of the day, your state of mind, your emotions and your spirit are all strong enough to give you the energy and vitality you need to go that extra mile. And beyond.

The 90s may be tough. But they're also incredibly exciting.

Use this book to power up... and enjoy every moment.

RECOMMENDED READING: *Perfect Health*, by Dr Deepak Chopra (Bantam Books); *Teach Yourself to Meditate*, by Eric Harrison (Simon & Schuster); *A Passion For Living*, by Dr John Tickell (Formbuilt).

10
HELPING OTHERS
TO HELP YOURSELF

We started this book talking about the stress in our lives. Many people are finding it tough — in all walks of life. And one of the things that's most lacking in our society today is support. We neither give much to, nor receive much from, others. It might be that people now just don't have the time to care, but it makes us all the poorer. From the Bible to the Buddhist sages, all say that what you give you will receive, or what goes around comes around.

Helping out friends, family and workmates should be a joy. And it's always good to know there's someone there ready to give you a hand if ever you need it.

However, giving support to others is a skill like any other. To genuinely be of help is quite different from merely offering... and making a half-hearted attempt. Often the greatest support you can give anyone is to listen to them. *Really* listen. So many of us go through our lives never feeling heard.

In order to be a good listener, it's necessary to follow a few simple rules:

First of all, pay attention to the environment you are both in. To get the most out of your time together, you must both be comfortable, relaxed and free from pressure. Also look at how closely you're sitting to the other person. The closer you sit, the more concentrated your attention will be. Don't get distracted by other things that may be going on around you, try to be absolutely focused on the other person, not on yourself.

Put your own feelings aside completely. You need to be totally objective about what you're being told. Check and double check what the other person is saying. Try to paraphrase in your own words to make absolutely sure you understand.

In addition, take careful note of what's *not* being said. Try to read between the lines.

Watch how the person holds themselves and their gestures. Body language experts believe that only ten per cent of what we are saying is verbal; the rest is in dress, expressions and posture.

People feel so much better when they believe someone has truly listened to them. If they decide to make changes in their life, support them. This can be a real test as we often don't want people we've become familiar with to change. We feel comfortable with them just the way they are.

If the other person is making life-changing decisions, encourage them to give some thought to managing their overall health as well. They could feel so much better if they were offered a few of the rules you've learnt about finding true health, vitality and happiness. Just little things like encouraging them to eat properly, or have an aroma-therapy oil bath to relax can help people through tough times.

But by far the greatest way of supporting anyone is loving them unconditionally. Even if we don't approve of, or agree with, what they are doing, we can still back them all the way.

PRACTICAL HELP

Sometimes we want to make a gesture of support but we don't want to impose. That's no excuse for standing back and doing nothing; instead, there are a number of ways of helping out without becoming an additional burden.

If a neighbour or close friend is struggling with a family, offer to take the children for a couple of hours to give them a break. You may never know how grateful they'll be. A member of your family may be leading such a hectic life that you know they never get the time to eat properly. Cook a little extra at dinnertime — they might really appreciate a little container full of food.

Put a bunch of flowers or a bottle of wine on the doorstep for a friend having a tough time. Send a bright card to someone you know is feeling down. Record a tape of relaxing music for a colleague you know whose heavy workload is causing sleepless nights.

Every couple needs a few hours of uninterrupted time together to keep their relationship healthy too. For some, this seems impossible. But how about offering to look after someone else's children for a couple of hours on a Friday night, so they can go out for a meal? Or taking it in turns to mind the children with another couple, to enable you to have an evening off occasionally?

These are all small displays of support that don't cost a lot yet which give people an invaluable boost when they most need it. The most important thing is showing that you care, and that those to whom you're giving a helping hand are well worth the time and trouble.

When you give someone support, you're increasing the other person's sense of self-worth and showing them they are valued. You are helping power them up and, in return, you'll be all the stronger. And healthier and happier too.

RECOMMENDED READING: *The Four Minute Sell*, by Janet Elsen (Arrow Books); *The Seven Habits of Highly Effective People*, by Stephen Covey (The Business Library).

Albert Ellis
Anger: How to live with and without it

Anger is one of the most damaging and fruitless of all
human emotions. Everyone is beset by the problems of
how to cope with it, how to live with it, and how to
understand it. Here is a solution to the problem of
anger; a solution that years of clinical testing and
research have proved effective. The breakthrough
technique of this book will enable you to challenge and
eliminate the anger that can frustrate and stand in the
way of your success and daily happiness in business,
in home life – anywhere you are – without losing your
assertiveness.

In this entirely new approach to coping with anger,
world-famous psychologist Dr Albert Ellis, founder of
the Institute for Rational-Emotive Therapy which now
has branches throughout the world, presents an easily
mastered, step-by-step technique that is designed
for you to perform on your own. It will help you
to systematically explore and, for the first time,
understand the roots and the nature of your own anger.

Dr Ellis does not merely present his own theory
and approach to anger. He compares his technique
to other, differing points of view. He gives you the
first comprehensive critical analysis of the various –
and often incompatible – approaches to the age-old
problem of anger, how to solve it and how to live
better.

Selwa Anthony with Jimmy Thomson
Succeed With Me

'Over the years I have seen all sorts of prescriptions for success. Some are a bit hard to swallow. Some have nasty side effects. Some just won't work for most people. *Succeed With Me* is a model for success that is as palatable as it is effective.

'With her contagious optimism, Selwa Anthony shows you how to focus on your goals, recognise your own achievements and build on your strengths.

'Believe me, when Selwa says *Succeed With Me*, it's an invitation worth accepting.'
DR KERRYN PHELPS

Leonie McMahon
Why Am I So Tired?

ENERGETIC, MOTIVATED, ACTIVE, FULL OF
LIFE...just some of the things we could all be if we
weren't so exhausted by twentieth-century living.

WHY AM I SO TIRED?
It's a question most of us ask ourselves at some time
or another, but because we accept fatigue as a fact of
life, it's not a question we really expect to find answers
to. Yet there are answers, and there are many simple
and effective ways of treating tiredness.

Leonie McMahon, a qualified chiropractor and
osteopath, acupuncturist, nutritionist, and homeopath,
with many years experience as a diagnostic clinician,
has drawn on her rich and varied background to
identify the physical, chemical and mental causes of
fatigue, which include:

* allergies * anaemia * boredom * candida
* glandular fever * incorrect posture
* overweight * pain * pelvic sprain
* repetitive strain injury * spinal curvature * stress
* unhappiness * vitamin deficiency

Once the cause has been identified, a solution can be
found, which could involve anything from a change in
diet to a course of acupuncture.

Tiredness *is* treatable, and with this practical, easy-to-
understand guide, you'll never again have to ask *Why
Am I So Tired?*

Dr Sandra Cabot
Women's Health

Combining the most advanced and up-to-date medical information with all the available nutritional and natural remedies, *Women's Health* is a guide to medical problems experienced by many Australian women at some stage in their lives.

Problems are analysed in clear, simple terms and, as well as presenting their causes, *Women's Health* also gives guidelines as to how particular conditions can be prevented from occurring in the first place.

PMS • period pains • breast and genital problems • sexually transmitted diseases • pregnancy problems • infertility • menopause • psychiatric disorders • skin disorders • obesity • sexual problems • contraception • arthritis • headaches • hormone therapy • osteoporosis • cancer • nutrional medicine

Dr Sandra Cabot, founder of the Women's Health Advisory Service in Australia, has written a book that women of all ages will find invaluable for their medical conditions and health in general. *Women's Health* has sold over 35,000 copies and is now revised and updated for the 1990s.